Life Savers

Written by Jo Windsor

Look at these life savers.
People have made them
to help us stay alive.

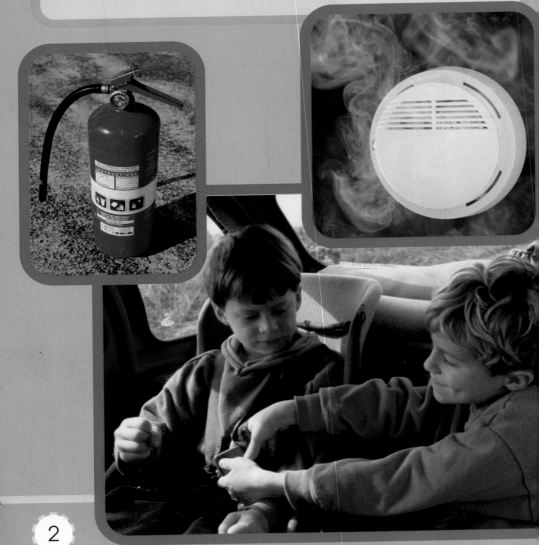

Look at this life saver.
The man is using it
to put out the fire.
It has foam inside.
The foam can
put out the fire.

fire extinguisher

This life saver is
a smoke alarm.
When a house is on fire,
a smoke alarm makes
a very big noise.
Firefighters come
to help put out the fire.

smoke alarm

Look at this seat.
It comes from a plane.
A pilot can make the seat
go up and out of the plane.
A parachute will help
the pilot come down.
This seat can help
a pilot stay alive.

ejector seat

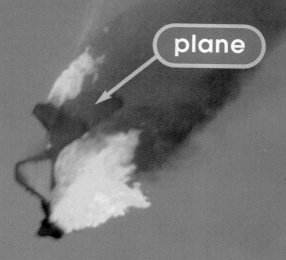

pilot

plane

Look at this car.
It has seat belts.
If there is a crash,
the seat belts can help
save your life.

seat belt

seat belt

This car has seat belts.
It has air bags, too.
The air bags will get big
if the car is in a crash.
The air bags can save
someone from getting hurt.

air bag

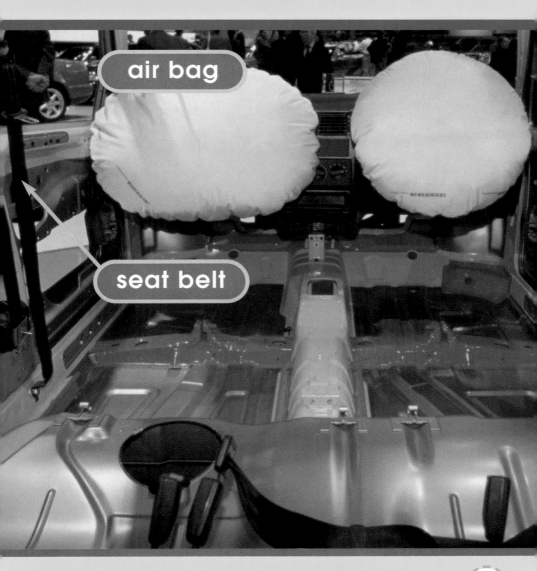

air bag

seat belt

Look at the little lights
on the road.
The lights are like cat's eyes.
They shine in the dark.
People can see where to
stay on the road.
The little lights can help us
to stay alive.

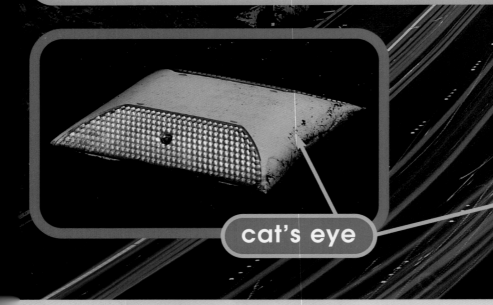

cat's eye

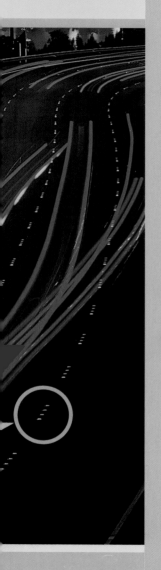

Index

Guide Notes

> **Title: Life Savers**
> **Stage:** Early (3) – Blue
>
> **Genre:** Nonfiction (Expository)
> **Approach:** Guided Reading
> **Processes:** Thinking Critically, Exploring Language, Processing Information
> **Written and Visual Focus:** Photographs (static images), Labels, Index

THINKING CRITICALLY
(sample questions)

- Look at the front cover and the title. Ask the children: "What do you think this book could be about?"
- Ask the children what life savers they know that can help save lives.
- Focus the children's attention on the Index. Ask: "What are you going to find out about in this book?"
- If you want to find out about a smoke alarm, on which page would you look?
- If you want to find out about seat belts, on which pages would you look?
- Look at pages 4 and 5. How do you think the foam puts the fire out?
- Look at pages 6 and 7. How does a smoke alarm help to save lives?
- What do you think could happen if you didn't wear a seat belt?
- How does an air bag help to save lives?

EXPLORING LANGUAGE

Terminology
Title, cover, photographs, author, photographers

Vocabulary
Interest words: life savers, alive, foam, smoke, alarm, pilot, crash, seat belts, air bags
High-frequency words (new): if, very
Compound word: firefighters
Positional words: up, in, on

Print Conventions
Capital letter for sentence beginnings, periods, commas